i

INTRODUCTION

As Ballistic Missile Defense (BMD) technology advances, the United States continues to move forward with plans to deploy hard-kill BMD systems to defend the United States homeland from attack. The most recent step in this endeavor will be the Initial Defensive Operation (IDO). When made operational this year, IDO will include the deployment of sea-based and land-based BMD systems in the Western Pacific region. The Bush Administration has stated in press releases that this deployment is for the purpose of defending the U.S. against a ballistic missile attack from a rogue nation,[1] and has since maintained that it is not meant to upset the balance of deterrence between the United States and other nuclear powers.[2] However, if not carefully counterbalanced IDO could threaten the People's Republic of China (PRC) by making the Chinese nuclear deterrent seem irrelevant. Such an action would upset the theater-strategic and national-strategic relationship that the United States has maintained so carefully with China. In order to avoid provoking Beijing while maintaining a cooperative United States-PRC relationship through IDO planning and deployment, Commander United States Pacific Command (CDRUSPACOM) should consider ways to counterbalance the negative message that IDO risks sending. USPACOM should increase communications and collaborative planning with the PRC, stepping up military-to-military relations to carefully and subtly show Beijing that overall United States policy toward China has not undergone a revolutionary change.

---

[1] *National Policy on Ballistic Missile Defense Fact Sheet*, White House Press Release, May 2003.

[2] *Inside the Pentagon*, 06 March, 2003.

This research paper describes the IDO in terms of what has been released in unclassified documents, and reviews the stated reasons for IDO. It reviews the balanced state of United States-Chinese cooperation by describing the evolution of the relationship over the past several decades, and it outlines the current strategic ambiguity that the United States maintains in its dealings with China. The important reasons for Washington's ambiguity is analyzed, in addition to the role United States ambiguity plays in regional stability. Regional and global consequences that could occur if Beijing misinterprets the IDO deployments are discussed. The risk of U.S. overcompensation is also reviewed; this counter-argument is discussed, with proposed mitigations. Finally, recommendations are made for USPACOM's engagement with the PRC to provide a measured counterbalance to any negative message Beijing receives from IDO.

This paper does not review the overall strategic advantages and drawbacks of the United States decision to withdrawal from the Anti-Ballistic Missile treaty. Furthermore, it is assumed that Washington's intentions are transparent with respect to the purpose of IDO and that national BMD systems deployed to the West Pacific are for the defense of the United States against a limited ballistic missile attack from a rogue nation.[3] As such, IDO does not represent a revolutionary change in United States policy towards China and is not part of a plan to nullify PRC's strategic deterrent and the Cold War concept of mutual assured destruction. Finally, the technical aspects of BMD will not be discussed, nor will some of the recent BMD mission-related concerns, such as command and control, communications or timely weapons release authority.

---

[3] Roy Eccleston, *Australian Washington Correspondent Newspaper,* (Sydney) 28 February, 2003.

FACTS

Initial Defensive Operations Defined

Initial Defensive Operations (IDO) refers to the deployment of BMD systems for the purpose of defending the United States homeland, or possibly an ally, against a limited ballistic missile attack by a rogue nation (i.e., DPRK). It is the latest evolutionary step in national missile defense, and is planned to be made operational in 2004. IDO will be comprised of the deployment of land and sea-based BMD systems in the Western Pacific, in addition to other land, sea, and space-based sensors.[4] Specifically, it will likely include Aegis BMD ships in the vicinity of Japan, equipped with the latest Standard Missile variant for maximum kinetic kill capability, and Patriot Advanced Capability missile systems, known as PAC-3, in Japan (which may possibly be used in both United States and Japanese defense).[5]

National BMD has gradually been introduced into United States defense policy in recent years as the available technology has made it more attainable. IDO is intended to be an evolutionary step towards national BMD. The National Missile Defense Act of 1999 (Public Law 106-38) states that "it is the policy of the United States to deploy as soon as is technologically possible an effective National Missile Defense system capable of defending the territory of the United States against limited ballistic missile attack (whether accidental, unauthorized, or deliberate)."[6] More recently, the policy stated in a White House Press

---

[4] *National Policy on Ballistic Missile Defense Fact Sheet*, White House Press Release, May 2003.

[5] David Pilling, *London Financial Times Newspaper*. (London), 16 January, 2004.

[6] *National Policy on Ballistic Missile Defense Fact Sheet*, White House Press Release, May 2003.

Release in May of 2003 was that "restructuring United States defense and deterrence capabilities to correspond to emerging threats remains one of the Administration's highest priorities, and the deployment of missile defenses remains an essential component of that broader effort."[7]

Development of the United States-Sino Balanced Relationship

The United States has maintained a position of delicately balanced strategic ambiguity with China for decades, and analysis of the current state of that balance plays a key role in dissecting possible PRC reactions to IDO. First, PRC concerns over United States intervention in the Chinese domestic matter of reunification of Taiwan with the mainland play a significant role in all Beijing decisions regarding the relationship with the United States. Additionally, the tight United States relationship with Japan, PRC human rights violations, and PRC proliferation of Weapons of Mass Destruction (WMD) are current significant issues impacting United States-Chinese relations.

United States policy on the Taiwan question has been of central concern in describing United States-PRC relations. Since the initial solidification of United States support for Taipei in 1954, with the creation of the United States-ROC Mutual Defense Treaty, United States policy toward the Taiwan question has seemingly reversed on several occasions. Taiwan was effectively used during the Cold War as a stronghold from which United States naval and air power could be employed in the event of war with China or the Soviet Union.[8]

---

[7] Ibid.

[8] John Garver, *Foreign Relations of the People's Republic of China*, (Upper Saddle River: Prentice-Hall, 1993): 51.

4

During the Nixon Administration, as a vehicle towards counter-balancing the Soviet Union, the United States entered an agreement entitled the United States-PRC Joint Communiqué on the Establishment of Diplomatic Relations, in which the United States acknowledged Beijing's 'One China' policy (to include Taiwan), but also reserved the right to maintain "cultural, commercial and other unofficial relations with the people of Taiwan." During the Carter Administration, in 1979 the United States normalized relations with the PRC, officially recognized Taipei as being under Beijing, agreed to remove all United States troops from Taiwan, and abandoned the United States-Taiwan defense treaty, then still in existence. To maintain some level of ambiguity, in that communiqué the United States still professed that it "continues to have an interest in the peaceful resolution of the Taiwan issue and expects that the Taiwan issue will be settled peacefully by the Chinese themselves."[9]

In 1982 the Reagan Administration again reversed course in United States policy by demonstrating United States commitment to Taiwan in stating "six assurances" that Taiwan could rely upon, which included United States refusal to acknowledge China's sovereignty over Taiwan, and indefinite United States arms sales to Taiwan.[10] One month later, President Reagan retreated into ambiguity when Washington and Beijing issued another Joint Communiqué, this one restating United States agreement with the One China policy, provided that Beijing agreed to "fundamentally" pursue peaceful solutions to the Taiwan question.[11]

---

[9] Rice, Darren, *Missile Defense for Taiwan: Implications for United States Security Interests in East Asia*, Thesis, Naval Postgraduate School, September, 2003: 38.

[10] "Six Assurances to Taiwan" in *Taiwan Documents Project* (Prexis Publishing, Los Angeles, 1999). Available from www.taiwandocuments.org/assurances.htm.

[11] Andrew Nathan and Robert Ross, *The Great Wall and the Empty Fortress: China's Search for Security*. (New York: W.W. Norton & Company, 1997): 58.

Through the 1980s and 1990s, United States sentiment grew more favorable toward Taiwan. Taipei's embrace of democracy, most notably in the legalization of opposing political parties, free newspapers, and continued movement toward free elections garnered increased United States support. Beijing's harsh suppression of all attempts at democratic reform, as typified by the 1989 Tiananmen Square Massacre, demonstrated the PRC's disregard for human rights, and as a consequence, American support for Taiwan grew, at one point culminating in the diversion of United States Naval aircraft carrier battle groups to the Taiwan area in support against PRC threats.[12]

In the latter half of the 1990s the United States continued to move toward Taiwan, while maintaining an ambiguous relationship with Beijing. The Clinton administration granted visitation to the United States for Taiwan President Lee Teng-hui in 1995, infuriating Beijing, which responded with three PRC military exercises designed to intimidate Taiwan during its Legislative and Presidential elections. Then, in 1999 the United States House of Representatives passed the Taiwan Security Enhancement Act (TSEA) as a means to support United States arms sales to Taiwan, and for United States and Taiwanese senior military officers to work together on threat analysis and doctrine, including Missile Defense. These actions further complicated U.S.-PRC relations. More recently, the relationship has again been frustrated by the April, 2001 U.S. EP-3-PRC F-8 aircraft collision incident.

Beijing's position on the Taiwan question can be summed up as follows: the PRC has made clear its strong desire to bring Taiwan back into the PRC (referred to as reunification) since the Chinese Civil Wars of the World War II era, and has been willing to consider

---

[12] "Taiwan: Recent Developments and United States Policy Choices," *Issue Brief for Congress*, (Congressional Research Service, 1 April 2003): 1.

almost any means to that end. Beijing has never completely abandoned the possible use of force across the Taiwan Straits as a prospect for achieving that goal.[13] As Taiwan has become more democratic to encourage greater acceptance by the world community, the PRC has refused to give up any ground in the debate, insisting that reunification is an internal Chinese matter and not open to United States influence or approval. PRC assimilation of Taiwan has evolved into a matter of pride and legitimacy for the Chinese Communist Party (CCP), as well as a matter of national sovereignty and respect.[14]

Close and solid United States relations with Japan also play a role in United States-PRC difficulties. All through the Cold War and since, Tokyo has followed Washington's lead in supporting Taipei's democratization and avoidance of reunification with mainland China. Moreover, Japan is well on the way towards enjoying joint missile defense with the United States. This agreement infuriates Beijing, as PRC's ballistic missile arsenal is certainly China's most significant deterrent against future Japanese aggression.[15] As a consequence, China remains suspicious of Japanese motives, despite Tokyo's following of United States engagement with China, its agreement to the "One China" policy in 1972, and its continued stated respect for that policy since. China still has very vivid memories of Japan's aggression during World War II, and does not maintain much faith in Japan's pledge to forswear militarism in the region.[16]

---

[13] Edward Timperlake and William Triplett, *Red Dragon Rising* (Washington D.C.: Regenery Publishing, 1999): 22.

[14] Rita Mathur, "TMD In the Asia-Pacific: A View From China," *Strategic Analysis: A Monthly Journal of the IDSA, 24no.8* (November 2000): 4.

[15] Ibid.

[16] S. Johnson and W. Lewis, *WMD: New Perspectives on Counterproliferation,* (Washington: National Defense University Press, 1998): 63.

Aside from the United States' alliances with Taiwan and Japan, the PRC's proliferation of WMD has also developed into a significant issue that undermines better United States-PRC relations. China has had a history of weapons and missile technology proliferation as part of its national security policy; it remains possible that China may resort to weapons proliferation in an attempt to counter United States policy decisions. Weapons transfers to Iran and Pakistan in particular have been problematic in recent years[17]. In July 2003 the United States decided to impose sanctions on five Chinese firms in response to contraventions of the Iran Non-Proliferation Act of 2000. One of the companies, Changgwang Sinyong, had been disciplined for previous violations in 1996, 1998, and 2000 for missile-specific export regulations. Since President Bush's inauguration in 2000, the United States has sanctioned China on eight separate occasions in response to proliferation violations.[18] China has also not embraced the Missile Technology Control Regime (MTCR)[19], which must be interpreted as an indication that Beijing still considers proliferation as an available diplomatic counterattack to United States policies.

United States-Sino Relations: The Current Balance

Today, USPACOM executes the current U.S. policy of intentional ambiguity toward the PRC as part of his theater-strategic responsibilities. USPACOM maintains a minimum level of military-to-military interaction with the People's Liberation Army (PLA) and the People's Liberation Army Navy (PLAN), while still maintaining technological support for

---

[17] Mohan Malik, "China Plays 'The Proliferation Card'." *Jane's Intelligence Review*, July 2000: 6.

[18] "US Arms Control/Nonproliferation Sanctions Against China," *Nuclear Threat Initiative*, www.nti.org, Internet. 02 January, 2004: 6.

[19] "Missile Technology Control Regime" *Nuclear Threat Initiative*. www.nti.org, Internet. 02 January, 2004: 1.

Taiwan. USPACOM shoulders much responsibility for tangibly maintaining United States relations with China, most specifically with respect to military-to-military relations, the quality and quantity of which convey a significant message of cooperation with the PRC. In his testimony to the House Foreign Relations Committee (HFRC) in 2003, ADM Fargo, CDRUSPACOM, described the current ambiguity in stating, "We have a modest but constructive military-to-military relationship with China. . . . . Our activities are part of ongoing DoD efforts to place such contacts with China on a new footing since the April 2001 aircraft collision incident."[20] The military-to-military relations to which ADM Fargo referred were the port visit of a U.S. Navy Aegis destroyer to Qingdao in November 2002, another DDG visit to Zhanjiang in September 2003, and the port visit of a Chinese warship to Guam in September 2003. ADM Fargo also visited China in December 2002, and the Chinese Minister of Defense visited USPACOM in December 2003.

In the same address to the HFRC cited above, ADM Fargo discussed United States support to Taiwan, stating, "We have worked this past year to support self defense improvements that can best meet Taiwan's identified defense needs."[21] Later, he further stated, "We want Taiwan to remain stable, democratic, and economically prosperous while it develops a professional, civilian-controlled defense establishment with a modernized, joint operations-oriented military."[22] His mention of engagement with both China and Taiwan is an indicator that the United States deliberate ambiguity policy remains the current.

---

[20] Fargo, Admiral, USN. United States Pacific Command Testimony to the United States House of Representatives International Relations Committee. June, 2003: 3.

[21] Ibid.

[22] Ibid.

Relations with the PRC have been progressing favorably since the EP-3 incident of two years ago, but no visible significant effort to step up engagement with the PRC has been made in the PACOM area of responsibility (AOR) in attempt to counterbalance the potential message sent by the IDO deployments.

ANALYSIS AND RECOMMENDATIONS

To best analyze the impact IDO deployments in the PACOM AOR may have on United States-PRC relations, it is important to address what is likely and also what may be possible in terms of reactions from Beijing. First, deliberate United States ambiguity is and will remain important for years to come and should not be abandoned as policy. Additionally, while the current United States administration views the IDO deployment as an intuitively obvious next step in national ballistic missile defense post-Cold War and post-September 11, 2001, it could be viewed by Beijing and the Chinese people as a revolutionary shift in United States policy and not an evolutionary one. That could upset the balance, and challenge China's security both from a regional point of view, as well as from a global-strategic perspective. China's receipt of such an unintended message could have significant consequences which may be largely unseen by the United States, to include the onset of another Cold War, as well as increased proliferation of WMD and delivery technologies. Overcompensating in embracing China too closely in attempt to maintain the balanced relationship through the planned IDO deployments however, would also have significant regional and global drawbacks to United States interests.

The Need for United States Ambiguity with China

United States ambiguity toward China remains the most favorable policy for U.S. interests, and this necessitates that IDO deployments in the Western Pacific region be carefully gauged and counterbalanced to prevent dramatically altering the fragile balance of the current U.S.-PRC relationship. This is especially true when viewed in the context of the varying degrees of friendship Washington has offered to China over the past several administrations. While the cyclic nature of Washington politics may serve to be a mitigating factor for inconsistency in foreign policy (especially in the American mindset), it may not always be viewed in a similar way by other cultures. By maintaining a "middle road" position in its relations with China, the United States plays a major role in maintaining regional stability. For this reason, the current U.S. course of action remains prudent and worth preserving; a plan that is restrained, yet positive in fostering limited cooperation, should remain the current U.S. policy goal.

Possible Misinterpretations – Tipping the Balance

The same BMD systems that the IDO deploys for the purpose of United States homeland defense and defense of our allies against DPRK attack, coincidentally, can also be perceived as nullifying China's nuclear deterrent, considering the regional threats that China faces, as well as its deterrence against United States hegemony. Such a perception, while seemingly paranoid to many Western observers, is viewed much differently by the Chinese. With recent U.S. incursions into Afghanistan and Pakistan, as well a temporary U.S. basing in Uzbekistan, Tajikistan, Thailand, and the Philippines, and permanent basing in South Korea and the Philippines, the PRC perceives itself as increasingly surrounded by a burgeoning U.S. worldwide empire. System capabilities of Aegis destroyer BMD will likely require IDO ship positioning somewhere north and east of the DPRK. With continued BMD

11

kinetic kill range and altitude improvements to existing U.S. anti-missile systems, from SM-2 Block IV to SM-3 to SM-3 Block 2, coupled with the fact that Beijing will not have precise knowledge of current U.S. BMD systems capabilities and limitations, it becomes reasonable for Beijing to conclude that minimal repositioning would enable the same U.S. BMD system to shoot down a Chinese ballistic missile launch. If such an IDO "threat" is perceived by China, it may have dire consequences for the fragile U.S.-PRC relationship.

Theater-Strategic Consequences

When viewed from a regional perspective in East Asia, China's misinterpretation of the IDO deployments would seriously disrupt PRC security. In the Beijing mindset, China's nuclear strike capability is its primary deterrent against the threat that its neighbors pose and it's primary means for influencing the debate over many disputed territories with which Beijing deals.[23] Furthermore, it is accepted by the Pentagon that Beijing's ballistic missile arsenals are the most formidable and coercive threat that both Japan and Taiwan face.[24] Any perceived diminution of its nuclear strength would likely drive Beijing to increase its conventional forces, potentially disrupting regional stability.

Global-Strategic and GWOT Consequences

From a global perspective, Beijing harbors some resentment over the perceived Western belief that China is not a first-world global player worthy of dignity. The PRC's emergence as a more influential and respected nation in the global community is a core goal of Beijing. Its efforts to realize these goals in the near and mid-term will certainly require a larger percentage of the world's resources, including oil, power and water for China, all of

---

[23] Mark Stokes, *Arms Control Today*, 33 no. 5, June 2003: 46.

[24] Rice, 18.

which necessitate that their security, and their ability to project power, be ensured. For the United States to communicate to the Chinese government and people, by either action or implication that it is America's intent to discourage Chinese development industrially and influentially, or to hamper their quality of life enhancements, is to reinforce the Chinese perception that perpetual United States global hegemony is Washington's real goal. A threatened China significantly increases the probably of future conflict, ultimately undermining U.S. security.

Tipping the balance of the relationship could also have a significant impact on the GWOT. If China senses that United States, or U.S.-Japanese, BMD IDO in the theater is meant to nullify the Chinese nuclear deterrent and isolate PRC regional influence, an isolated China is more likely to act in its self-interests alone, selling technology and materials to other countries and non-state actors seeking WMD as a counter to U.S. global influence. Such PRC action would have global consequences, threatening the stability of nearly every region.

Consequences of Overcompensation

Conversely, overcompensating for IDO by being conciliatory to Beijing could be just as destabilizing as an isolated and threatened China. Overt friendship, coupled with support to China would send a message to Japan, Taiwan, Indonesia, South Korea and other regional nations that the United States does not stand with them against potential PRC regional aggression. These nations already remain leery that the United States would not go to war with China in effort to repel Chinese aggression against their national interests. Any significant thaw in U.S.-PRC relations could encourage these countries to provide for their own strategic defense by withdrawing from the Nuclear Non-Proliferation Treaty of 1968 (NNPT) and pursuing their own nuclear weapons programs, which is well within their technological reach. From the point of view of those countries, the benefit NNPT membership provides in nuclear power generation assistance and oversight may no longer be sufficient motivation to refrain from building nuclear weapons. Today the main reason these countries do not develop their own programs is because the United States assures them that it will provide for their strategic defense. Japanese, South Korean, Indonesian or Taiwanese withdrawal from the NNPT would increase the probability of nuclear conflict in East Asia and, in turn, ultimately reducing regional and global stability. Overcompensation also risks undercutting U.S. moral authority to protest to human rights' violations in China and around the world. Any United States move toward China to counterbalance IDO must be carefully considered and subtle to avoid tipping the worldwide nuclear balance.

Subtle Counterbalance Ensures the Correct Message is Received

In order to best communicate to Beijing that the current balanced relationship with the United States must be maintained for the continued well-being of both nations, USPACOM should consider purposefully benign and subtle ways of moving the relationship forward on some fronts, in an effort to counterbalance the perceived move toward PRC isolation that IDO risks prompting. By increasing military-to-military interaction with the People's Liberation Army and Navy (PLA-N), and expanding port visits, collaborative planning, and low-level Encounter Exercises (ENCOUNTEREX) United States forces in the PACOM AOR could subtly reinforce a cordial United States-PRC relationship, while also being mutually beneficial to both countries. While this small move closer to the PRC risks upsetting United States relationships with other regional partners, a measured approach could mitigate adverse consequences.

In addition to routine United States Navy port visits to Hong Kong, the two recent port visits to Zhanjiang and Qingdao fostered enhanced U.S.-PRC ties, and the frequency of such visits could be increased with United States State Department and Beijing approval. Moreover, USN ship visits are routinely received warmly by local Chinese politicians due to the money that is injected into the local economies for channel transit and inport ship's services, as well as money that servicemen spend while in port. Similarly, PLA-N ship visits to United States ports could increase, to include a greater number of visits to Guam, Hawaii and West Coast ports, offering partnership while expanding trust among greater numbers of PLA-N officers who feel comfortable interacting with USN personnel and systems.

A second possibility for ensuring that Beijing does not misinterpret IDO is to establish a habit of conducting simple tactical exercises between USN and PLA-N ships on a annual or semi-annual basis. Since the end of the Cold War, the United States Navy has operated with the Russian Navy on several occasions with much success. Complex operations would not be necessary, and the actual conduct of the exercise would not need to be much beyond the most rudimentary level. Similar exercises with other regional countries normally include such simple events as shiphandling drills, helicopter over-the-horizon targeting, international signal flags drills and formation steaming for a photograph opportunity. Such an approach would provide a largely benign way of establishing basic military-to-military relationships. A collateral benefit would be that these exercises would enable the United States to better understand PLA-N systems, fundamental fleet movements and operations.

Finally, the planning that occurs for the above exercises, coupled with an increase in the number of U.S.-PRC Flag Officer visits, would communicate on many levels that relations between the two governments are not eroding, but remain steady.

COUNTERPOINT AND MITIGATIONS

The potential drawback of these recommendations that requires discussion is that concerned regional countries leery of Chinese aggression may sense that the United States is embracing China too closely, disrupting regional stability and encouraging them to build up their own conventional forces and nuclear arsenals as noted earlier. That is unlikely if the interactions suggested are kept low-key, informal and benign. For mitigation, any risk of misinterpretation occurring could be tempered if the United States communicates to concerned nations, in a transparent manner, the reason for the increase in U.S.-PRC interaction. As the United States conducts more port visits, increases military-to-military interaction, and initiates low-level naval exercises with China, USPACOM and the Department of State would need to make clear to regional partners that this does not discount their treaties with the United States, but is meant to dissuade China from misinterpreting BMD deployments and disrupting regional stability. The Chinese ballistic missile deterrent with the United States has been a building block of regional stability in the Western Pacific and South Asia for decades, alleviating the PRC's need to develop an excessive conventional force. With such an approach, regional countries are likely to recognize the important role China's deterrent continues to play in regional stability, and will be more encouraged to support United States efforts to prevent IDO from disrupting the balance.

CONCLUSION

The menace posed by the unpredictable and potentially volatile DPRK regime, with its vast military capabilities, coupled with the threats emergent from the Global War on Terrorism, necessitate that the United States protects itself as quickly as possible. IDO will go a long way to offering that protection, and as a collateral benefit will provide a deployed and operational platform to evaluate and modify presently unresolved challenges (i.e., command and control architecture, communications, release authority coupled with response time, etc.) to help shape the BMD mission area and the security it provides for the future. However, it is important that the U.S. Government and USPACOM, in particular, make clear that IDO is not intended undermine China's security. In the absence of a shift in national policy with respect to China, USPACOM must ensure that its actions in the region do not communicate the wrong message. IDO implementation must therefore be accompanied by a deliberate and subtle campaign to embrace the PRC as suggested in this paper. If the United States takes steps that alienate China, by either action or apathy, and provoke Beijing's sense of isolation, then the probability of a second Cold War will grow as the PRC rearms itself and shares its threatening technology to counter a perceived U.S. military hegemony.

Selected Bibliography

"Defense Watch." *Defense Daily* 219, no. 23. (November 3, 2003): ProQuest Direct Database. Accessed: 21 November 2003.

"Defense Watch." *Defense Daily* 210, no. 6. (April 9, 2001): ProQuest Direct Database. Accessed 21 November 2003.

"Executive Summary of Report to Congress on Implementation of the Taiwan Relations Act." *Defenselink.* 18 December 2000.ProQuest Direct Database. Accessed 21 December, 2003.

"Missile Technology Control Regime (MTCR)." *Nuclear Threat Initiative.* 26 March 2003. ProQuest Direct Database. Accessed 21 December, 2003.

"National Policy on Ballistic Missile Defense Fact Sheet." 20 May 2003. Available from www.whitehouse.gov/news/releases/2003/05/20030520-15.html Internet. 28 November, 2003.

"Six Assurances to Taiwan." in *Taiwan Documents Project.* (Prexis Publishing, Los Angeles, 1999). Available from www.taiwandocuments.org/assurances.htm. Internet. 21 January, 2004.

"United States Arms Control/Nonproliferation Sanctions Against China," *Nuclear Threat Initiative*, 31 July 2003, ProQuest Direct Database. Accessed 21 December, 2003.

"United States, Japan Review Options for Future Sea-Based Missile Network." *Defense Daily International* 2, no. 36. (Jul 12, 2002): ProQuest Direct Database. Accessed 22 November 2003.

Armacost, Michael and Kenneth Pyle. *Japan and the Engagement of China: Challenges for United States Policy.* 12, No. 5, (December 2001).

Carter, Jimmy. *Keeping Faith.* New York: Bantam Books, 1982.

Christensen, Thomas. "The Contemporary Security Dilemma: Deterring a Taiwan Conflict." *The Washington Quarterly*, 25, No. 4, (Autumn 2002).

Christoffersen, Gaye. "The Role of East Asia in Sino-American Relations." *Asia Survey.* Vol. 42, No. 3. (May/June 2002).

Cronin, Patrick and Michael Green. *The United States-Japan Alliance: Past, Present, and Future.* New York: Council on Foreign Relations, 1999.

Fargo, Admiral, USN. United States Pacific Command Testimony to the United States House of Representatives International Relations Committee. June, 2003.

Finkelstein, David. *Washington's Taiwan Dilemma, 1949-1950*. Fairfax: George Mason University Press, 1993.

Garver, John. *Foreign Relations of the People's Republic of China*. Mass: Prentice-Hall, 1993.

Johnson, S. and W. Lewis. *WMD: New Perspectives on Counterproliferation*, Washington: National Defense University Press, 1998.

Malik, Mohan. "China Plays 'The Proliferation Card'." *Jane's Intelligence Review*, July 2000.

Mann, Paul. "Strategic Reconnaissance at Issue in Sino-United States Tiff." *Aviation Week and Space Technology* 154, no.15. (April 9, 2001): ProQuest Direct Database. Accessed 22 November 2003.

Mathur, Rita. "TMD In the Asia-Pacific: A View From China". *Strategic Analysis: A Monthly Journal of the IDSA*. 24, no. 8 (November, 2000)

May, Greg. "China's Opposition to TMD is More About Politics than Missiles." *Global Beat*. February 2000. Available from www.nyu.edu/globalbeat/usdefense/ May0200.html. Internet. Accessed 06 Januaty, 2004.

Nathan, Andrew and Robert Ross. *The Great Wall and the Empty Fortress: China's Search for Security*. New York: W.W. Norton & Company, 1997.

Porch, Douglass. "The Taiwan Strait Crisis of 1996: Strategic Implications for the United States Navy." *Naval War College Review*, 52, No. 3, 1999.

Rice, Darren, "Missile Defense for Taiwan: Implications for United States Security Interests in East Asia". Masters Thesis, Naval Postgraduate School. September, 2003.

Smith, David. "Sun Tzu and the Modern Art of Countering Missile Defense." *Jane's Intelligence Review*, Asia: 12, No. 1, (1 January 2000). ProQuest Direct Database. Accessed 22 November, 2003.

Spence, Jonathan. *The Search for Modern China*. New York: W.W. Norton, 1999.

Timperlake, Edward and William Triplett. *Red Dragon Rising*. Washington D.C.: Regenery Publishing, 1999.

Wang, T.Y. "Taiwan and Theater Missile Defense." *The Journal of Social, Political, and Economic Studies*, Washington (Fall 2000).

Yuan, Hong. "The Implication of TMD System in Japan to China's Security." *Chinese Academy of Social Sciences*. 1998. Available from www.nautilus.org/library/security/ papers/Hong_Yuan-EngISODARCO.PDF. Internet. 06 January, 2004.

Zhao, Quansheng. "The Beijing-Tokyo-Washington Triangle." In Marie Söderberg ed. *Chinese-Japanese Relations in the Twenty-first Century: Complementarity and Conflict*. London: Routledge, 2002.

Zhongqi, Pan. "The Dilemma of Deterrence: US Strategic Ambiguity Policy and its Implications for the Taiwan Strait." *The Henry L. Stimson Center*, 2001.